a Nick Myra Mystery

CONFESSIONS
of a SECRET SANTA

by BRYCE MORGAN

Illustrated by KEVIN TERRY

M5 Productions
Buckeye, AZ

ISBN 9798339101574

M5 Productions
Buckeye, AZ

Cover Design: Bryce Morgan

CHAPTER 1:
'TWAS THE NIGHT BEFORE CHRISTMAS

ate was afraid. But as he dashed through the back alleyway, faster than he'd ever run before, he realized that he couldn't just run away. He needed his brain as well as his feet at a time like this. He needed to be smarter than the average eleven-year-old. He had just seen something he wasn't supposed to see, and now he was being chased by two men he didn't know. The first man's footsteps weren't far behind him, and a tire squeal just seconds earlier seemed to confirm that the other man was driving to intercept him where the alleyway ended, right across from Brewster's Deli. The chain link fence Nate had peered through moments ago, that fence the first man was forced to climb, had given the boy a decent head start. But if he tried to avoid the street (and van!) ahead and escape down a longer, adjacent alley to his left, the first man would probably catch up to him. "Think!" he told himself.

Nate Washington was no stranger to this area. For several years now he had lived on these streets and regularly explored these back alleys. Over time he learned which places were safe, and which ones were not. He learned when and where to sleep. He learned when and where 'expired' food was thrown out. He learned how to blend into a school group on a field trip. He learned

how to avoid the case workers who only wanted to send him back to a foster home. Maybe other kids had good experiences with a foster family. Nate had not. He and his friends— other kids like him, kids he met in places like the park and library—took their chances on the streets of New York City. And they looked out for

each other. One of those friends was Alex, the boy he had just seen through the fence; the boy that, shockingly, he had just seen tossed into the back of that van. But when the wooden crate Nate was standing on started to crack under his weight, the two goons, illuminated by the van's headlights, realized someone was watching them. There was a witness to the abduction, and that someone was him. So when the first man pointed and shouted to his partner, Nate ran.

But in spite of his fear, and what seemed to be a hopeless situation, Nate remembered a small gap between two buildings not far ahead. It was just narrow enough that most people took no notice of it. But it was just wide enough for a kid his size to squeeze through. It would dump him out across from the park, a familiar place with lots of good hiding spots. As he hit the corner wall of this narrow passage with his left shoulder, he took note of the old piping and utility boxes that dotted each side of the gap. He wanted to slide through as fast as he could without

getting his clothes snagged. But halfway down the gap, he suddenly heard the grunting of the first man. His pursuer, apparently skinnier than Nate imagined, was now pressing himself through the narrow passage as well. The man was straining every inch of the way, but getting frighteningly closer. As Nate quickened his pace, he fixed his gaze beyond the narrow divide. He could see the park's west gate and its trees, which were  presently silhouetted by a display of Christmas lights not far beyond the fence line. At this point on that cold Christmas Eve, he could even hear holiday music rising up from the same illuminated display. With the first man closer than ever, Nate finally popped out the other side of the gap. He was ready to bolt as fast as he could across the street, toward the park fence and the holiday crowd deeper in. But emerging from the tight passage, headlights suddenly blinded his eyes, and the sound of squealing tires filled his ears. With his arm now shielding his view, Nate was at a standstill, frozen by the fearful idea that somehow the second man, the van driver, had also known about the narrow gap and beat him to the spot.

CHAPTER 2:
DASHING... IN A
ONE-HORSE OPEN SLEIGH

s Nate shifted his head out of the path of the headlights, he realized it wasn't the thugs' van that had cut him off, but a large, red sedan with a white top. It was, in fact, a 1972 Cadillac Eldorado convertible. Not that Nate knew the vehicle's make and model. But he did recognize the van, which had just rounded the corner at the end of the block. He could also hear the first man's straining groans getting louder behind him. But who was in this red car? Was it a friend of the pursuing goons? He still felt paralyzed to act. Then the passenger window of the sedan dropped and a voice bellowed out, "Come with me if you want to live!"

As the driver of the Cadillac leaned closer to the open window, Nate could make out the round face of a stout, older man with a pure white beard

and a sculpted tuft of white hair on his head. The intensity of his introductory command, still visible on his face, suddenly shifted to a jolly expression.

"I'm guessing that was a little over the top," the stranger said, shifting his eyes to the side with a kind of uncertain regret. He spoke again, regret replaced by reassurance. "Kid, it's either them or me. Don't worry. It'll be okay. Now hop in."

Somehow, in an instant, Nate knew he was right. As the passenger door swung open, the young man launched himself into the car. The tires squealed again as they made their escape.

"So who are those guys chasing you?" the stranger asked.

"I... I don't know," Nate said looking nervously over his shoulder. "I think they were trying to kidnap me."

"Kidnap you? Why would you say that?"

"They took my friend Alex," Nate confessed reluctantly. "And... other kids we know have gone missing over the past few months."

The bearded driver stared straight ahead, looking pained. "Oh my." He turned to Nate. "Good thing we got..." His words were interrupted by shots ringing out and bullets whizzing by their vehicle. The bad guys' van had reappeared and was bearing down on them... along with gunfire!

"Ho-ho-holy smokes", the stranger stammered. "Hold on!" He made a hard right turn in an attempt to elude the determined thugs. But as Nate peered back over the leather seat, he saw the van had made the turn as well.

"We need to get to the police station," the man announced while checking the rear view mirror.

"But you're going the wrong way. The 4th Precinct is down Delaney," advised Nate (having learned the places it was always better to avoid).

"No, there's another one right up here," the man calmly responded.

Suddenly, a different kind of loud noise followed one of the gunshots, a sound that came from the back of the car. "They shot the back tire,"

exclaimed Nate. The louder, closer, and lower sound repeated itself. "They got the other one," Nate announced anxiously.

"Not to worry. This Caddy has an 8.2 liter V-8 engine. Even with just two tires, they won't catch us," the stranger said confidently. But after two more quick turns, and more gunshots, the same sound and jolt was coming from the front of the Cadillac as well.

"What were you saying about 'just two tires'?" Nate asked, with both fear and frustration in his voice.

As the man attempted one turn after the other, it was clear the car was slowing down and getting harder to steer. Nate knew they couldn't keep going like this. Soon, the plain white van would catch up with them, along with the goons and guns it was carrying.

CHAPTER 3:
A LITTLE OLD DRIVER, SO LIVELY AND QUICK

s the Cadillac roughly rounded the next corner on four flat tires, the stranger seemed more interested in inspecting Nate's seat than keeping his eyes on the road.

"Hey, where's your seat belt?" the stout driver suddenly blurted out. "Did you know every year..."

"Look out," Nate shouted as they almost collided with a slow-moving car.

With a few quick twists of the steering wheel, somehow the large, red 'land yacht' narrowly avoided the smaller and slower vehicle in their path. "Okay, put on that seat belt. The precinct is just around the next corner," announced the stranger, "and we'll be coming in hot."

As bullets continued to whiz by their car, Nate could feel the already rough ride getting even rougher. This coincided with loud thuds coming from the wheel wells. Though the young man didn't know it, the vehicle's tires were beginning to shred. As the Caddy began to transition from rubber tires to metal rims, Nate could see sparks flying up from underneath, and he could hear the grinding noise growing louder and louder inside the vehicle.

"Hold on!" the man shouted, as he veered into the rightmost lane and slammed on the brakes. They were definitely coming up on a police station, since not far ahead of them, Nate  could see several police cruisers parked out front... police cruisers they would soon slam into if they didn't stop in time. Nate covered his eyes, convinced they were too close and going too fast to avoid a collision.

But suddenly it was quiet. Nate opened his eyes to find a police cruiser only inches in front of the Cadillac's bumper and the stranger hanging out the driver's side window as the goons' van rocketed past.

 "Hah! Guess who just got their plate number," the man proudly exclaimed.

As Nate, still shaking from the experience, looked back to his right, he saw the front facade of the 12th Precinct. He still couldn't figure out why they had not gone to a closer precinct, but after the goons and the guns and the nerve-racking car chase, he was strangely glad to see a police station. He suddenly felt a hand on his shivering shoulder. He looked over at the stranger's kind face.

"Why don't we get inside and let them know what happened," the man calmly suggested.

As they walked up to and into the precinct house, Nate was able get a better look at his rescuer. As he noted earlier, the man was large, but not pudgy. The white hair on his head, along with his white beard, were set against a deep red (or crimson) winter coat, with a similarly-colored suit underneath. He moved confidently for a man his age, and there was a look of quiet determination in his eyes. As for his voice, Nate sensed some kind of accent, but it didn't sound like any accent he'd ever heard (even growing up in a melting-pot like New York City).

Once inside, Nate kept his distance as the stranger interacted with the desk sergeant. After a minute, he finally moved closer in order to find out what was happening.

"If you need to talk specifically with Detective Alonso, it will be a few minutes," the sergeant explained. Nate's new friend simply nodded as he turned and gestured to Nate, his eyes locked on a row of chairs against the wall.

"Anyone can help us, right?. So why are we waiting for that guy?" Nate asked, not wanting to spend longer at the station than was necessary.

"I've heard he's the best. Worth the wait," the man explained.

Nate looked puzzled. "But we need to do something *now*. Those guys were going to kill us. And they have Alex!"

"That's why we need someone who will get things done. I think Detective Alonso is our man," said the stranger in red.

"Pff," Nate puffed dismissively. "They're all the same. They're all just..."

"Cops?" a voice questioned from a doorway to their right. Yep. It was Detective Alonso, and he didn't look happy.

CHAPTER 4:
IT'S CHRISTMAS TIME IN THE CITY

Even if what you're saying really happened," Detective Alonso said bluntly, "the first thing you need to do is fill out a report."

Resenting the suspicion (and the detective's overall grumpiness), Nate piped up. "Whaddya mean 'if'? The car's right out front, with four shot-out tires! People must have heard the gunfire."

"Kid, no one's going door-to-door asking people if they heard loud noises on Christmas Eve just because your car has four flat tires. And as for your friend being abducted, and the other kids you mentioned, I think we'd know if a bunch of children were disappearing," Detective Alonso responded.

"Not if they were kids no one cared about anyway," Nate remarked with disdain.

"Now wait a minute. We..." Alonso began in protest.

The stranger quickly inserted himself. "Detective, you're Jason Alonso."

"Your point, Mister, um, Mister...?" the detective said, now searching.

"Mr. Myra. But you can just call me 'Nick'," the stranger replied. "And my point is that I and others remember the headlines. You're the one who

tracked down the 'Southside Snatcher'. You also exposed that couple, the Reynolds, the 'Foster Accosters' who were hurting all those kids. You care about children, Detective, that much is clear."

Instead of being positively influenced by Nick's praise, Jason Alonso seemed to become more detached... and even more determined to end the conversation. "Mr. Myra... Nick, that was a long time ago and things change. But one thing that hasn't changed... the process. Fill out a report! We'll take it from there. Good night, fellas."

Detective Alonso was already turning away as those final words left his lips. As he did, Nick gently caught his arm. "Detective. Thank you for seeing us. Please take my card, just in case. I'll be sure to leave all the relevant information with the officer on duty, including that license plate number." Nick handed him a red and white business card. "And Detective Alonso," said the man in red as he began to take his first step backward.

"Yes, Mr. Myra?" Alonso asked, exasperated.

"Merry Christmas," offered Nick warmly.

The detective maintained his detached expression. "As I said, good night, fellas." And with that, Jason Alonso pressed his shoulder through a nearby door and disappeared from sight.

"See. He doesn't care. None of them do," Nate argued, his hand upturned and outstretched toward the door through which the detective exited.

"He does. The pace of Providence can be mysterious, Nate. We'll have to be patient," Nick replied as he slowly moved back toward the desk sergeant.

Nate was thoroughly confused. "Provi-what? What are you talking about? We're running outta time. We can't just do nothing."

"Not to worry. We're already doing something," Nick explained. "Now tell me if there's anything else you remember about those men; anything they did or said that might provide a clue. Anything at all could be helpful."

The young man looked down, his eyes shifting from side to side as he thought. "Actually," Nate said calmly as he looked back up, "there was something I didn't mention. But first, why don't you tell me how you know my name."

CHAPTER 5:
SINCE WE'VE
NO PLACE TO GO

ate was growing impatient. The stranger, Nick, had not answered his question. Instead, Nate had to wait around while the man filled out the police report. Thinking about what had happened up to that point, the young man felt sure he had never once mentioned his name. But somehow, the man in red knew it. What was he not telling Nate? Was it really safe to stay with this "Mr. Myra"? Maybe he should just stay at the station or make a run for it once they stepped outside. But when they finally did, Nate decided to press the question again. And yet, as the precinct doors closed behind them, Nick spoke up first.

"Nate, thank you very much for your patience," he said with a reassuring sincerity. "I know you must be wondering if you can trust me, since it seems like I haven't told you the whole story. I would be wondering the same thing if I was in your shoes, young man."

"But you still haven't answered my question," Nate said nervously. He had been grateful for Nick's help, and (for some reason) had believed the man when he said earlier it would be okay. But he also knew from real life, from experience, that people were not always what they appeared to be; that people lied, and not everyone could be trusted.

"I know your name," explained Nick, "because I didn't just happen to drive by when those men were chasing you."

"So you're working with them?" Nate asked.

"No, of course not. Why would they be shooting at us if I was working with them?"

"I don't know," blurted Nate. "Maybe it's part of some big scheme, to get me to trust you. Or maybe you're the competition, and you just got your hands on me first."

"Or maybe I'm a tiny space alien driving a robot that looks like an old man, and I'm here to take you to my flying saucer, which is currently hovering over the Empire State Building," Nick suggested with a twinkle in his eyes.

Nate was not amused, and simply stood there glaring up at the man.

"Okay. Too much. I get it. My point is that all those stories are very hard to believe. The truth is actually simple: I became aware of your situation and was trying to locate you. As I was doing exactly that I happened to see you running from those men. When I saw you cut in between the buildings, I sped up to meet you on the other side. I'm just glad I got there before they did."

"But why? Why were you looking for me in the first place? Why do you even care? You don't know me," Nate said, curious, but clearly guarded.

"Because that's what I do. I help kids who are in trouble," Nick calmly responded, with his same reassuring sincerity.

Nate wasn't sure what to say. He believed what Nick was telling him, but there were still so many unanswered questions.

"I promise I will tell you more," Nick said while pulling out and looking at a silver pocket watch that had been tucked inside his coat, "but we're running out of time. I need to know what else you remember."

Finally deciding it was better to trust Nick than go out on his own, Nate spoke up. "Okay. I remember one of the men chasing me was wearing a jacket, and it had something like a one-eyed dog on the back, with some words underneath. I think one of the words was 'security'."

"Hmm. Maybe a logo for a company," Nick proposed. "I think I know who can help us, and they're not far away; thankfully, within walking distance."

As Nate and Nick walked briskly away from the precinct house, they were unaware of two men watching them from a shadow-covered alley across the street... two men sitting in a plain white van.

The man with the jacket pulled out a cell phone. "Yeah. Tell the Broker that the kid and the old man just left the station, and they're headed uptown."

CHAPTER 6:
YOU'RE A MEAN ONE, MR. GRINCH

Jason Alonso was hunched over, his head on his desk, when the desk sergeant dropped a stack of files on the opposite side.

The detective slowly lifted his head. "Can't you see I'm taking a power nap?"

"Can't you see it's Christmas Eve? I've got family at my house as we speak, so I'm outta here," explained the desk sergeant, with squinted eyes and a smirk on his face. "Here are the latest reports, including that one from the old man with the kid."

Alonso let out a sarcastic sigh. "Wonderful."

Across the room, an older officer who was explaining to a new transfer the precinct's filing system, piped up after noticing Detective Alonso's lack of Christmas cheer. "What's wrong, Mr. Scrooge, too many 'Christmas crazies'?"

"O'Connell, don't you have someplace else to be? Like eating a fruitcake with your mother-in-law?" Alonso responded gruffly.

"Ha ha, Ebenezer. Yes, once I finish with Maxwell here, I'll make like a Christmas tree and 'leave' you to your holiday stupor," O'Connell explained.

"I think you mean, needles, O'Connell. Christmas trees have needles... 'needle-less' to say," Alonso said with a pleased look on his face (though his head was still barely lifted).

Maxwell, the new transfer, spoke up, curious about the cranky cop across the room. "Is that Jason Alonso, the one who was on TV and in the newspaper back in the day?" he whispered.

"Yeah, that's him. At least what's left of him."

"Wow. What's the story? He seemed to be going places back then," remarked Maxwell.

"He was," O'Connell replied. "Somewhere under that crabby shell is a really good cop. But things changed when his wife and kid died a number of years back. He hasn't been the same since."

"That's awful." said Maxwell, now looking across the room with pity. "Sad story. His wife struggled with mental health issues and drugs. One

day, she ups and takes off with the kid. Alonso looked for them for a couple years. Finally followed her trail to a condemned apartment building. But that same building had been the scene of a terrible fire, just a few days earlier. Fire department said two of the victims were a woman and child about those same ages."

"Man, that's tough," Maxwell replied, shaking his lowered head.

"Yeah, Alonso was crushed. Who wouldn't be? Like I said, he hasn't been the same since. He gets his work done alright, but usually just creeps along with, ya know, ho–hum kinds of cases. Zero ambition. But like I said, he gets his work done alright. That's why the Captain keeps him on."

At almost that same moment, Captain Carlyle came walking out of his office. Though the Captain was oblivious to O'Connell's mention of him, he wasn't oblivious to Alonso's so-called "power nap".

"Alonso!" the Captain barked across the room.

"Yes, Captain?" Detective Alonso responded, far faster than his sluggish posture would lead anyone to expect.

"Do you need something to do? It's the season of giving, and I'm feeling extremely generous."

"No, Captain. I'm... um... I'm just waiting on a plate number search... for a possible 'road rage' incident," Alonso explained, trying his best to look engaged.

Though the Captain looked skeptical, he turned his attention to a group of officers loading up presents for a local toy drive. As he turned away, Alonso grabbed the file containing Nick's report and quickly entered the

plate number listed there. In an attempt to look somewhat busy, Detective Alonso 'studied' the results of the search. As he casually scanned down the screen, his face and posture began to change from forced focus to genuine interest.

"Hmm," Alonso thought to himself, looking back at Nick's report, and then back to the screen. "Hmm. Maybe the old man isn't 'Christmas crazy' after all."

CHAPTER 7:
CHRISTMASES LONG, LONG AGO

ick *Myra*. What kind of name is 'Myra' anyway?" Nate asked as they walked through a quieter neighborhood of large, brownstone homes about fifteen minutes from the police precinct.

"It's the name of my hometown... though I was actually born in a town not far from there," Nick replied, scanning the homes as he went. "And what about your last name? I didn't catch it."

"It's 'Washington'. Nate Washington," said the young man, zipping his jacket up a little higher.

"Ah, yes. Washington, just like the city park."

"That's right," Nate said somewhat defensively, "like the park. And like the President."

"Washington. Washington," Nick repeated, thinking hard as he looked up. "I remember George Washington having a camel brought to Mount Vernon on Christmas in 1787. Funny the things you remember at Christmastime. Well, Nate Washington... welcome to the Lepps."

As the older man gestured, the younger man's gaze was caught by a beautiful, multi-storied row house rising up right in front of them. Not only was its architecture impressive, but the extensive holiday lighting and the warm glow that emanated from every window was absolutely entrancing.

After knocking several times, a young girl (about Nate's age) answered the door.

"I'm not supposed to open the door to strangers, but I saw you through the glass," she said, looking at Nick, "and I thought you were bringing presents early." Nate just smiled at the pretty girl, oblivious to her words.

"I'm sorry to disappoint you, young lady, but I'm actually here to see your *vanavanaema*," Nick replied. "And... I'm guessing you already have presents under the tree."

The girl smiled to the affirmative. "Yes, but I'd gladly accept more. Come in. You look like you could be one of *vanavanaema's* friends."

"I certainly am, from a long time ago."

"Her room is on the top floor, last door on the right," she said, gesturing to the staircase. "I have cookies I need to finish decorating." And with that, she ran off toward the back of the house, where the voices of others could be heard enjoying the holiday.

As Nick and Nate arrived at the top of the staircase, they detected soft music and holiday smells floating down from a door at the end of the hall. Nick slowly opened the door, revealing a room lit by many, many candles, and full of old things, things made of dark wood, patterned glass, and rich leather. And in the far corner sat a very old woman looking over a photo album, with a thick blanket over her legs.

"Tere. Kas me võime sisse tulla?" Nick asked softly, in perfect Estonian.

"Jah, muidugi. Kes see on?" the woman asked in response.

"It's an old friend, Riina." Nick replied in English. "I told you I'd see you again one day."

"Come closer, so I can see you," said the woman, her accent evident.

As Nick knelt down next to her chair, her hands slowly moved to hold his face. Astonished, she greeted him. "*Jouluvana*! How long has it been?"

"A very long time, Riina. And as I told you then, please call me Nigulas," he said graciously. "This is Nate. He and his friends are in trouble, and I'm trying to help them."

The woman had a hard time turning her joyful eyes from Nick. But she finally did and looked at Nate with a warm smile. "I'm glad you're here, Nate. Please know that you can trust *Jouluvana*. He was there for me when I was a little girl, not much younger than you. When I was scared and wanted to give up, he reminded me that we are never alone. There is always hope. I know he will help you as well."

Nate wasn't sure how to respond. Not only did he feel awkward (the way kids can sometimes feel awkward around older people), but he was confused by Nick's relationship to this woman.

"Um. Thank you," Nate replied. "So you and Nick were childhood friends?"

"No, child," the woman said, turning back to cup Nick's bearded face. "He was then... just as he is now. How could I ever forget him?"

CHAPTER 8:
SOMEBODY
WAITS FOR YOU

ate sat with Nick on a low but long bench in the entryway of the Lepp's home. Riina, the great-grandmother, had grown tired, and she and Nick had said their tearful goodbyes. But not before Riina had called for her son, Magus. He was the one for whom the two visitors now waited. As the minutes passed, Nate occasionally looked over at his new companion, trying to make sense of what he had heard upstairs. Nick, who was cheerfully taking in the front living room and formal dining room, with all their holiday décor, finally noticed the boy's curious gaze.

"It sure would be nice to live in a place like this, don't you think?" Nick proposed to his bench-mate.

"I don't know," said Nate. "On a cold night, sure. But I think I'd feel pretty cooped up."

"Of course. But you do know the 'freedom' of the streets comes at a cost, right?" suggested Nick. "Isn't there someone out there looking for you?"

"My situation's only temporary," responded Nate reassuringly.

"My parents and I got separated for a little while, but they're coming back for me. And until they do, I can take care of myself."

Nick smiled and returned his gaze to the Christmas decorations. "Yes, I'm sure you can."

The two sat in silence for another minute, until Nick added a closing thought. "Remember, Nate, there's nothing wrong with wanting to be with your family; with your parents again. It really is okay to miss them... and need them."

Not only did Nate begin to squirm, he also began to form the words he needed to defend the idea that he really could take care of himself. But as he turned to argue his point, a large, serious-looking man came walking down the stairs. This must be Magus Lepp, Riina's son.

"Mr. Myra, I presume," said Magus as he extended his hand (though his face was still smile-less).

"Yes, Mr. Lepp. Nick Myra. This is my young friend Nate. Thank you so much for having us in your lovely home."

"Well, any friend of my mother's is welcome here. She asked me to help you in whatever way I can. So... how can I help you gentlemen?"

Nick cleared his throat. "I'm aware that you own the largest private security company in the city."

"That is correct. We are fortunate to have a long list of clients," Lepp responded, looking slightly uncomfortable with talking about his success.

"I'm actually more interested in your competition," offered Nick, as he raised an eyebrow. "Do you happen to know of a local security company that has a one-eyed dog on its logo?"

"Come to think of it, I do. I think it's actually a wolf with one eye," said Magus. Nate, who was a bit intimidated by the man, now stepped closer with rekindled curiosity.

"It's a small outfit called Rching Security. They're a newer group. I'm pretty sure they're based in the Randolph Building down on Payne Street, just above that large toy store."

Nick's smile grew larger. "That's very, very helpful."

"Mr. Myra, if you have a security need, I'd be more than happy to have some of my men contact you. We do offer exceptional service, and I'd make sure there was no cost involved," Magus offered.

"That's extremely generous of you, but no. We're not in need of any security services," turning to look at Nate with a wink and chuckle, "at least not at this point in the night." Nate rolled his eyes.

Magus Lepp remained smile-less. "Well, I'm glad the information was helpful. Please make sure to take some cookies before you go," Magus said as he turned for a plate on a nearby end table. "I told my granddaughter I would make sure you received the ones she decorated."

"Oh, I do love cookies at Christmas," Nick replied, scooping up three or four, before turning toward the door. "And thank you again for your help. I pray you and your family have a very, very blessed Christmas. Please let your mother know again how wonderful it was to see her."

"I certainly will. Good night, and Merry Christmas."

As Nate stepped back into the cold night air, his mind raced with thoughts about his friend Alex, the men who chased him, and the one-eyed wolf. And somewhere deep inside of him, he could feel the troubling grip of a very different kind of chill.

CHAPTER 9:
WHILE I TELL OF YULETIDE TREASURE

n other places this kind of small grocery store might be called a *convenience store*. But in this city it's a *bodega*. And the bodega into which Nick pulled Nate was particularly busy (probably with people who had forgotten something important for their Christmas Eve festivities).

"Hey, what are you doing?" groaned Nate. "This isn't the Randolph Building."

"You're very perceptive," Nick shot back as they wove their way through stressed shoppers, his eyes fixed on the rear of the store. "I'm pretty sure we picked up a tail. Hopefully we can lose him by going out the back way."

"A tail?" said a confused Nate. He looked down at the back of Nick's coat, wondering if he'd see some stray streamer dangling there.

Nick noticed his eyes. "No, a 'tail' like someone following us. I wasn't sure before, but after leaving the Lepps, I think I caught sight of him in a couple window reflections; and when I bent down to tie my shoe a few blocks back. I hate to say it, but it's probably one of the guys from that van."

Nate became visibly shaken. He anxiously looked back over his shoulder. "How could they know where we are?"

"They may have waited for us to leave the police station," Nick suggested. "But fear not, young Mr. Washington. Here's our 'escape hatch'." The older man suddenly took a hard right through a set of colorful curtains, past several supply room shelves, and out the bodega's back delivery door. As they stood in the back alley, Nick spotted a smaller, adjoining alley. "Hurry! Let's cut down that way," he said in a loudish whisper.

After a couple tense minutes of weaving down side streets and alleyways, the pair emerged across from an old church. Nate continued to scan nervously in every direction.

"Don't worry. I think we lost him. But thankfully, we aren't lost! This is exactly where we need to be. Come on," Nick said as he urged Nate across the street with a hand on his back.

As a Christmas Eve service was letting out near the front of the historic church, the pair quietly slipped through a side gate leading to the back of the building. After quickly making sure there was no one around, Nick stepped off the path and made his way to the rear corner of the old chapel. He knelt down and began to dislodge grass and dirt around one of the foundation stones.

"What the heck are you doing?" Nate whispered as he knelt down, while also looking toward the people milling about up front.

As Nick cleared away a good amount of dirt, Nate began to make out edges that revealed the cornerstone was even smaller than he first thought.

Then the older man, grabbing both edges, began to do something surprising: he was actually trying to pull the stone out from under the building. And would you believe it... he did! As Nick brought the newly freed stone into the light (light shining from two church windows above them), the boy could see the brick had been hollowed out. And in that hollowed out space, something was wrapped up.

"Speaking of George Washington, did you know this chapel is where he worshiped regularly, including on the day of his inauguration as president," Nick remarked as he removed the folded cloth.

Nate was thoroughly confused. "What is that? And what does any of this have to do with finding Alex?"

"If we're going to get into the Randolph Building after hours, I only know one person who can help us. And... I only know one thing that might actually persuade him to help us. And a long time ago, I left it here."

As Nick unfolded the cloth, Nate could see it contained a number of coins, a pair of old glasses, a necklace, a slim book, and a small piece of stamped paper. "This church was built around 1765, right around the time of the British Stamp Act. It was almost by accident I left this stamp in here. I never guessed it would become so valuable... or... that it might just help us find your friend."

CHAPTER 10:
CITY SIDEWALKS, BUSY SIDEWALKS

hy not just wait for a taxi or rideshare?" Nate asked as he and Nick quickly descended the subway station steps.

"It's Christmas Eve, Nate. More people are going places, but less drivers are working tonight. We just don't have time to wait around," Nick explained. "But not to worry. The J Train will get us there in no time. So I guess "J" is for "joy," his grin widening as he looked around for a good place to stand.

Again, Nate rolled his eyes as he breathed out an exasperated sigh. Given how serious (and if he was honest, how scary) their situation was, and how far they seemed to be from finding Alex (and maybe the other kids), he couldn't understand why this strange (and strangely familiar) old man acted the way he did; staying so...positive. Didn't he understand how bad things really were?

"By the way," added Nick, "did you know the first subway system was built in London in the 1850s and 60s? But oh boy, believe you me, some of those original lines did not have the best ventilation."

As the first sounds of the approaching train began wafting down the tunnel, Nate noticed a large group of men (and some women) flooding onto the platform. This group was hard to ignore, not simply because of their numbers, but because they were all dressed like Santa Claus.

The group started to fill in the space around he and Nick, and not surprisingly, his new companion let out a chuckle of delight as he began to scan  the bearded crowd. From the group's conversations (including one between Nick and a very short, Asian Santa), Nate learned that all of them had been collecting last-minute donations throughout the city. Apparently, this charity work was followed by a 'Santa dinner' held somewhere nearby. That's all Nate was able to make out before train sounds drowned out the chatter. But as each person's attention began to turn to the newly arrived subway cars, Nate caught a glimpse of Nick in this 'sea of Santas'. He couldn't have known then that, though his mind was presently consumed with the alarming events of the evening, the scene would be an image that would stay with him for the rest of his life.

When (a short ride later) they finally returned to street level, Nate recognized the neighborhood. It was Chinatown, with its tall, but narrow signs full of foreign letters, and its countless cords strung high across the street (from which dangled traditional lanterns in a variety of colors). No sooner had they crossed the street than Nate's jolly companion was talking with a street vendor... in what must have been Chinese!

"He said the building we're looking for is just a block over," explained Nick as he launched out.

Not only was Nate surprised by another conversation in a foreign language, but also afterward, by how hard he had to work to keep up with his white-haired partner. Three back alleys later, the two stood in front of a nondescript door painted to match the dark color of the building, and thus, a door that was difficult to see at night. The only thing that stood out was a doormat laying at its base. On the doormat, in large, dirty letters, was the phrase, "Go Away". Though Nate couldn't see it, somehow, to the right of the door, Nick found a button. He pushed it, but there was no accompanying sound to indicate it was working. Moments later a garbled voice rang out from a hidden (and obviously run-down) speaker.

"Can't you read? Go away!" the voice barked.

"Gao. I'm an old friend of your dad from Qinghai. Maybe he mentioned me? Nick Myra?"

After at least twenty seconds of silence, the speaker crackled again. "Step onto the mat so I can get a better look at you," the man instructed. Nate leaned in and looked up. Sure enough, there was a small, darkly-colored camera in a corner above the door.

As Nick stepped forward onto the doormat, a muffled, mechanical clicking could be heard underneath it. After looking down to his feet, he looked back

at Nate, and then to the camera above.

"Unless you want this to be your last Christmas, I would suggest staying perfectly still," the voice gleefully recommended. "The explosives underneath that mat can be a bit unpredictable."

CHAPTER 11:
CHRISTMAS EVE WILL FIND YOU

xcept for a dimly-lit bulb above the door, the "Schraeder & Sons" storefront was dark. After knocking several times, Detective Jason Alonso moved over to the front window, cupping his hands around

his eyes and pressing his forehead against the glass. The interior of the plumbing supply store seemed just as dark as the sidewalk outside. One didn't have to be an NYPD detective to figure out why. A simple, hand-written note was taped in the bottom-left corner of the window: "Closed Christmas Eve and Christmas Day. Happy Holidays!" Though this was the Queens home address listed on the police report, it was clear that no one was present to answer his questions.

Alonso shrugged as he walked back to his vehicle. "Just as well.

At least it gave me a good reason to get out of the precinct for a while, and away from the Captain's generous, Christmas spirit," he thought to himself.

As he passed by the alley just next to the hair salon (that was just next to "Schraeder & Sons"), he caught the faint sound of what sounded like holiday music. Curious, he moved quietly down the alleyway, and eventually behind the storefronts. There, on the backside of the plumbing supply store, was a small garage with what looked to be an apartment built over it. Just inside the garage, to the melody of a well-known Christmas song, an older man was humming along as he toiled under a vehicle's hood.

"Good evening, sir," Alonso said carefully, hoping not to startle the man. The merry mechanic didn't budge. "Good evening, sir," he stated again, this time in a louder voice.

"Oh, good evening," the man replied, peeking up from just above the car's radiator. "Merry Christmas! How can I help you?"

"I'm here about the van you reported stolen," the detective explained.

"No, it's no longer available. It was stolen," the man responded while still gazing down and turning what Alonso assumed was a wrench.

"Yes, I know it was stolen. I'm a detective with the NYPD. I was hoping to ask you a few questions."

"Yes, I did report it to the NYPD, but I don't know about any detective," the man said with a confused look on his face.

Alonso was getting frustrated. Just before he made a third attempt at explaining who he was and why he was there, he decided turning the music down would improve his chances. So he walked to an old 'boom box' radio sitting on the man's very cluttered workbench and did just that.

"Hey. That's one of my favorites," the man protested.

"Mr. Schraeder, I presume?" Alonso asked as he mustered a smile that looked somewhat sincere.

"Yep. That's me. Didn't catch your name though."

"I'm Detective Jason Alonso with the NYPD," pulling back his coat to reveal his badge. "I wanted to ask you some questions about the van you reported stolen a few weeks ago."

"Sure thing. Did they find it? Since I hadn't heard anything, I just assumed it was gone for good," Mr. Schraeder offered.

"Allegedly, it was seen this evening, in connection with a 'road rage' incident," Alonso explained.

"Oh no. That's awful. It was a good vehicle for a lot of years. My son and I responded to a lot of plumbing calls in that van. After he died, it just sat... for a very long time. So what happens when I finally get around to selling it? It gets stolen! If I could find those two guys who took it, you better believe I'd give them a piece of my mind."

"Two guys?" Alonso interrupted. "The report didn't say anything about two guys. Did you see who took it?"

"Well, like I told the officer who took the report—and who seemed like he had better things to do—my old security camera caught them in the act."

CHAPTER 12:
OUR FINEST
GIFTS WE BRING

s the mechanical clicking continued, Nate looked down at the doormat with terror in his eyes, then took two steps back. "Did he just say explosives?"

Nick remained calm and lifted a reassuring hand to his young companion. "Gao? There's no need for the theatrics. Like I said, I was a friend of your father's back in China. Maybe he taught you the saying, "When Nick knocks..."?

Within seconds, the crackling, open line could be heard through the speaker again. Finally the man spoke haltingly.

"When... Nick knocks... and the... tick tocks..."

"Then open the door more," replied Nick,

"And heed the need," Gao said more confidently as he finished the saying.

"Yes, yes! You've got it. Now... would you literally 'open the door'?" asked Nick.

"Definitely sounds different in Mandarin," the speaker announced,

followed by a long pause. Suddenly the clicking noise that could be heard beneath the doormat stopped, a loud but short buzzing sounded, and an automatic lock on the door whirred open.

As he began to push the darkly-painted door ajar, Nick turned back to Nate, who by this time had backed up most of the way across the alley.

"I think we've sorted it out. Come on in, young Mr. Washington," Nick said warmly.

"Sorted it out? He was about to blow you up! How is a guy like this supposed to help us?" asked Nate as he shook his head.

"You'll see. C'mon," Nick whispered as he stepped through the door and held it open. Slowly, Nate made his way in and up a flight of stairs (that were just as dimly lit as the entryway). As the pair rounded the corner into the upstairs space, Nate felt like he stepped into the cluttered storage room for some kind of classic electronics museum. Shelf after shelf, floor to ceiling, contained what looked to be old computers, radios, phones, and various other devices Nate didn't recognize. As they moved through these stacks to the better-lit corner of the room, the Christmas Eve companions could hear someone muttering under their breath. As they emerged from the rows of shelves, they saw a middle-aged, Asian man frantically sorting through papers as he cycled his gaze between at least ten different video and computer screens. After mumbling a few more frustrated phrases, he finally noticed the strangers.

"Can't be too careful you know. Lots of people would like to shut me down. Others want to learn my secrets. Just can't be too careful. So what 'need' must I 'heed', Mr. Nick? My dad talked about you. Oh yes. And, ha ha, you look just like he described. Strange." As Gao spoke his eyes would regularly dart back to his screens and papers. "He said if you came I should help you.

No matter what. But 'Guerrilla Gao' is a busy man. And in demand, if you know what I mean."

"Of course. I knew that to be true," Nick replied, amused by the man's frenzied pace. "I also know you are an avid philatelist." He leaned over toward Nate and said in a whisper, "That's a stamp collector". Returning his gaze to Gao, he pulled the cloth from his pocket. "That's why I've brought you this as a gift." Nick opened the cloth and produced the small, stamped paper Nate had seen earlier.

Once Gao caught sight of Nick's offering his frantic demeanor quickly drained away. He looked up at Nick's smiling face with skepticism on his own. Grabbing a pair of gloves, he carefully took the stamp from Nick's hand, then moved to a lit magnifying lens on a nearby workbench.

"A colonial Almanac Stamp. I'd say 1765. I've never seen one in this condition," breathed Gao, as if in love. "Okay. What do you want for it Mr. 'Nick Knocks'?"

"As I said, a gift. A Christmas gift! But if your unmatched computer skills could produce for us an all-access entry card for the Randolph Building, we'd be incredibly grateful."

CHAPTER 13:
QUIET AS A MOUSE, DIDN'T MAKE A SOUND

hough it was less than 40-stories tall, the Randolph Building had become an iconic part of the midtown skyline. Built in the early 1930s, the Art-deco edifice was indeed stunning, but it was best known for the large "Toy Box" sign built on its roof. The massive neon sign could be seen from almost everywhere in the nearby park and down several major streets as one looked westward. Its bright red, electric letters towered next to an equally massive toy chest, overflowing with over-sized, classic toys of all kinds. New Yorkers had come to love not only the sign, but the annual 'Gift Exchange', in which a helicopter would carefully remove the giant toy chest and replace it with an equally large Christmas present, complete with unique wrapping paper each year and topped off by a huge bow. That same evening, the new holiday installation would then be illuminated in a festive ceremony in front of the sprawling toy store that occupied the building's lowest levels.

In the fading hours of this particular Christmas Eve, the Randolph Building had become the setting for an unfolding mystery. Below the upper level offices of companies on holiday break, the toy store itself had closed several hours earlier after saying goodbye to a crowd of last-minute shoppers. But the locked doors were no obstacle for Guerilla Gao's access card. So through the half-lit aisleways of the toy store, Nick and Nate cautiously crept, watching for any security guards who might be making the late-night rounds.

"Gao said the floor plan showed a stairwell in that back corner," whispered Nick to his young friend.

Nate was hardly paying attention. Though he so often tried to act older than his age (which his life-circumstances usually demanded), he was still just a kid. And like any kid in a massive toy store that's been decked out for the holidays, he was slightly distracted.

"Ooh. My friend Jada found some of these Christmas poppers last year in a dumpster. They're so fun. Messy, but fun," remarked Nate as he grabbed a handful from a nearby bin.

"Why don't you return those and we'll find that stairwell instead," Nick advised with a smile Nate sighed and reluctantly turned back to the sale bin before the pair continued on. Within minutes Gao's counterfeit card had allowed them to access not only the stairwell and the building's upper levels, but also the Rching security office. And yet, after hastily searching every room for the missing kids, the duo found nothing. So they decided to look for anything that might indicate where the children had been taken.

As Nate went from desk to desk looking through papers, he eventually called out to Nick. "Did you find anything yet about Alex and the others?" he asked anxiously.

"Unfortunately not. Lots of client files, employee files, invoices; stuff you'd expect to find. The only thing I can't make sense of are these medical supply invoices in a file folder for the annual 'Gift Exchange'. Probably just misfiled. Or maybe in case there's an accident? Not sure. What about you?"

"Beyond not knowing what I should be looking for, I don't see anything super weird... except a secretary who's obsessed with Santa." Nate was shaking his head as he looked over the festive but cluttered desk; a workspace that was

covered with Santa figurines, snow globes, and a tiny North Pole village. Strangely, one snow globe in particular caught his attention. It included a classic red convertible with a white-bearded driver sporting sunglasses and a Hawaiian shirt. Two surfboards were poking out from the convertible's back seat. A small nameplate on the globe's front read, "Surfin' Santa". But it was the tiny car's tiny California license plate that jolted Nate. It simply said, "ST NICK". Suddenly, something was unlocked in Nate's mind, and the pieces of that nagging feeling began to fit together. It began to make sense of how he just appeared out of nowhere. The red car. The red coat. The bushy, white beard. How he knew things. How he spoke so many languages. How he seemed way older than was possible. Even the way he reacted to those cookies! Nate dashed across the office, certain, but uncertain.

"You!" Nate shouted as he ran up to Nick. "Why didn't you tell me you're Santa Claus?"

CHAPTER 14:
WHO'S GOT A BEARD THAT'S LONG AND WHITE?

anta Claus?" Nick asked with a look of exaggerated shock. "Apart from the white beard, red coat, rosy cheeks, and husky build, how could anyone ever mistake me for Santa Claus?" His look of disbelief quickly morphed into a smile.

"Very funny," replied Nate. "But as usual, you didn't answer my question."

"Okay, Sherlock Holmes. Tell me why Santa is so famous, especially this time of year?"

"He's famous because he delivers toys on Christmas to kids all over the world."

"Exactly," responded Nick calmly. "Now, do I look like I'm getting ready for a trip around the world? As we stand here in this dimly lit office, even if I had a list, does it look like I'm 'checking it twice'? If I was leaving shortly to drop down chimneys on every continent in order to bless children, would I be running around New York City at this late hour with just one kid?"

Nate look confused. This 'supposed Santa' had a point. If Nick was Santa, it seemed unlikely that he was the Santa Claus with whom Nate (and most of the world) was familiar.

"Okay. I guess not," muttered a frustrated Nate. "But your name's Nick, like "St. Nick". And duh... you *look* like Santa Claus! And you speak all these languages. And you know all these people. And the cookies. And... and," Nate said as his excitement grew, "somehow you're way older than is possible. If you're not Santa Claus, who are you?"

"Well, that's a complicated question," answered Nick, now looking up and stroking his beard. He looked back at Nate, then away, then back at Nate, as if he was trying to figure out if the young man could be trusted. "I don't tell every child this, but I think you, young sir, can handle the truth."

"What truth?" Nate asked, slightly cocking his head to the left, like a curious puppy.

"The truth that on my last birthday I turned one thousand, seven hundred and fifty-four years old," Nick responded, with his signature grin.

"What? How? How is that possible?" Nate asked, eyes as wide as Christmas cookies.

"It's possible because long ago I asked God for more time. And would you believe it, he gave it to me. As I told you, I come from a town called Myra. As a pastor there, I especially loved to help the children and young people in that region. As is true today (and sadly, always has been true), there were so many needs; so many kids who were suffering. When I got to be the age that I appear to be right now, I sensed the story of my life was fast approaching its final pages. And so I prayed a bold prayer. I asked God to extend my life just

a little longer, so I could help even more
children. The night I prayed was Christmas
Eve. Now, do you know what happened
after I fell asleep that night?"

Nate, who had been hanging on Nick's
every word, quickly responded. "No. What
happened?"

"I woke up seven days later, on the very first day of the new year. But
surprisingly, I didn't wake up in my home. I didn't even wake up in Myra. I
found myself far away, in a strange land, where I didn't know a single person

or even how to speak the language. But as I
learned the language of that land, I also learned
there were children in need among them. Over
time, I understood that I had been placed there
for that very reason; as I told you earlier, 'to help
kids who are in trouble'. But I figured out quickly
that my window to help is somewhat narrow.
Even though my original prayer was simply for

a little more time, that very next Christmas, the same thing happened. I
fell asleep in one place and woke up, the following year, someplace completely
different. And in each location, from year to year, I
learned how to carry out my divinely-gifted mission."

"So that's how you helped Miss Lepp? You woke
up in Estonia when she was a little girl?" Nate asked,
genuinely trying to put the pieces together in his head.

"Yes, exactly. And Gao's father was just over a
decade later. And as you might have guessed, this
year I woke up here again, in New York City. Why?
Well, that's where you come in, Nate Washington."

CHAPTER 15:
IT'S THE
LITTLE SAINT NICK

 get it," Nate exclaimed, while continuing to work out Nick's stunning revelation. "This year you woke up here, to help Alex and the other kids, right?"

"Yes, something like that," answered Nick. "Throughout the year, I help kids in lots of little ways. But there's always something bigger; some larger mission I discover along the way."

"But how," Nate asked, slowly shaking his lowered head. "How can you help kids in all of these strange places if you're just like me?"

Nick seemed genuinely confused. "Like you? What do you mean?"

"I mean when you wake up in a new place, you don't even have a bed, or a home, or a bank account. But wait. You do have a car... or at least you did. And you do have nice clothes. And... okay. Hmm. Maybe I don't get it," Nate concluded, as he shrugged his shoulders.

"Trust me," replied Nick, "I felt the same way for the first few decades of my global adventure. I wasn't sure how to make it all work. But wherever

I woke up I always seemed to be led to kind people who helped me in a variety of ways. Some gave me a place to sleep. Others provided food or a way to earn a living. Still others helped me learn the local language. After many years, I also noticed something else. I noticed that once in a while, I would wake up in a location I had visited decades earlier (or at least, someplace nearby). After this happened several times, I began to stash away items of value; things that might help me if I returned to the area."

"Like the hollow stone under the church," Nate said excitedly.

"Yes, exactly. And as the world has become more connected over the centuries, it's been much easier for me to access resources I've collected throughout the years. But there's something far better than these resources; even better than the knowledge I've acquired from generation to generation. My most valuable possessions are the relationships I've been given. You see, I have an extensive, local friends network all over the world. It's composed of people I've helped when they were children, along with their children, and their children's children."

"That's how Gao knew about you, right?" Nate asked.

"That's right! I often teach kids a little saying, like a secret code, something they share with their family members, and one day, their own children. They learn that just as I've helped them, someday, I might also need help. And believe you me, that network has come to my rescue countless times

over the centuries. In fact, there was one time about a thousand years ago in the Chola Kingdom of southern India that I..."

"But how do you remember it all? Is it because you're Saint Nicholas?" Nate interrupted. "All those people and places and secret stashes. My brain already hurts just thinking about your story."

"That's a good question. No, I don't have any special 'saint' powers, and... between you and me, I've never really liked that title. Let's just say that early on some very helpful teachers showed me some very helpful ways to re-member lots and lots of things. But right now I think what's most important to remember is this: we're running out of time," Nick gently suggested. "Wouldn't you agree?"

With that, Nate seemed to snap out of his understandable fascination with Nick's story. "Yes," Nate agreed sadly. "And we're no closer to finding Alex and..."

To Nate's utter amazement, no sooner had his friend's name slipped from his lips than all of the office lights suddenly flickered to life, and Alex himself was visible at the far end of the room. Unfortunately, Alex was not alone. The two goons from the alleyway, the two goons who had abducted Nate's friend,

the two goons who had shot at Nick's car, were standing with Alex, guns drawn.

"Well look who we have here, Joey. It's like a Christmas miracle. We spend all this time looking for them, and they end up here, like presents under the tree."

"I suggest you let the boy go, gentlemen," Nick said sternly.

"Save it, pops. You can work it out with the Broker. That's right. He'll be here any minute."

CHAPTER 16:
A THRILL OF HOPE, THE WEARY WORLD REJOICES

r. Schraeder carefully positioned the old television set on the work-bench. He then proceeded to dig through a box of old cables, one stacked nearby on the cluttered, garage floor. Detective Alonso stood at the far end of the workbench and checked his watch.

"Give me just a minute," Mr. Schraeder requested as he pulled up handfuls of old video cords. "After the van was stolen, I decided to update my security cameras. But later, when I finally pulled all the old wiring, I got sidetracked by this car repair. I guess for a guy who felt the need to upgrade his security, I'm now even less secure." Mr. Schraeder chuckled and shook his head.

"I guess so," remarked Alonso, staring blankly out into the alley just beyond the old garage doors.

"So you got stuck working the Christmas Eve shift," Mr. Schraeder commented as he worked to connect a cable to the back of the old television.

"I bet your family isn't happy about that."

"Actually there's a holiday bonus for working tonight, so I usually request it. And no, there's no family to worry about," the detective responded, in a noticeably detached tone.

Schraeder stopped his fiddling. "No family, heh? Sorry to hear that. It might still be in the cards for a young guy like you."

"It was in the cards. I just got dealt a bad hand," Alonso replied looking directly at the older man, that detached tone now visible in his gaze. "But that's over now. So... how's it coming with the video system? I'd really like to see that security footage."

"Almost got it. Let me just find the tape," Mr. Schraeder said as he opened up another box. "Sorry to hear about that 'bad hand'. You know, you may have some 'clogged pipes' as a result."

"What?" asked a confused Alonso, now himself fiddling with the television's power cord. "'Clogged pipes'? Is that some kind of plumbing metaphor?"

"Exactly," replied a bright-eyed Mr. Schraeder. "When my son died, things

were all clogged up inside of me. I looked and sounded like you. I stopped caring because caring hurt too much. But one day (call it a vision, call it my vivid imagination), I saw my son right over there by that storage locker, holding a bottle of drain cleaner. But on the label it didn't say 'drain clear'. It said 'hope'. I knew that's what I needed, and that it was what my son would want for me." With an old video cassette tape in hand, Schraeder walked over and stood uncomfortably close to his guest. "If there's any way you can get a taste of hope, Detective, I know that would help free some things up inside of you."

For just a brief moment, Jason Alonso looked into the older man's eyes and seemed to entertain the idea of change. But his face hardened once again.

"I'm sorry for your loss, Mr. Schraeder. But I'm here on police business, not for therapy. Now... is that the tape we're looking for?"

Though his elderly host was a bit deflated, his smile remained. He placed his free hand on the detective's shoulder and calmly said, "Yes. This is exactly what we've been looking for."

"Well let's take a look. It's getting late and I wouldn't want to keep you from your work," responded Alsonso coolly.

Mr. Schraeder pulled up a tattered stool and switched everything on. After inserting the cassette, he advanced the tape to the time of the incident. Alonso checked his watch again.

"Here they are. You see, they came in from the next street over."

Alonso leaned in toward the old monitor. Two men were clearly visible. One man seemed to be the lookout as the other attempted to gain access to the locked van. As the 'lookout' turned to peer down an adjacent alley, Alonso spoke up.

"Pause it there."

"Do you see something?" asked Mr. Schraeder.

"Yep. That jacket with the wolf on the back. It's too dark and grainy to make out the letters underneath, but I know what it says," Alonso remarked, shaking his head. "It says 'Rching Security'."

CHAPTER 17:
YOU'RE AS
CHARMING AS AN EEL

he two goons were telling the truth. Nick and Nate stood in the Rching office with guns pointed at them for less than a minute before the Broker arrived. And when he walked through the back door, two more goons accompanied him. Nate wasn't sure what the title 'broker' meant, but it was clear from the thugs' earlier comments (and their present posture) that this man was indeed in charge. And yet, the man looked disconcertingly normal, not like the associate of men who abduct children. His appearance was like one of the many businessmen Nate would often see

in the nicer parts of the city. He wasn't tall, but he was slender. He wasn't young, but he still had a good head of hair; dark hair slicked back and perfectly kept. The only thing that really stood out about the man were his glasses. They looked very old-fashioned, like the small, round frames Nate had seen in photos from a hundred years ago.

As he walked in and noticed Nick and Nate, he didn't flinch at the sight

of the two uninvited guests. He whispered something in one of the goons' ears, before approaching the captive pair.

"Well, I'd like to say that you two were nothing more than a minor annoyance. But you've delayed my timeline, and that simply isn't acceptable," the man announced coolly.

"Oh my," blurted Nick, with a tone of genuine remorse. "We didn't know we were interrupting your holiday plans. The two young men and I would be more than happy to depart and let you gentlemen get back to your dealings."

"I'm afraid it's a bit late for that, Mister..." the Broker remarked, then inquired.

"Mr. Myra. Nick Myra. And you are?" asked Nick.

"I'm the man who is removing you and your friend here from the equation."

Nate's face hardened. "So that's it? You're just gonna kill us?"

"Kill you? What kind of a monster do you think I am, young man? We're simply calling the police."

"I don't get it. If the police come, they'll see what's happening here," Nick warned.

"I'm not sure what you mean, Mr. Myra. What exactly is happening here? We'll simply let them know about two individuals who illegally entered our office, and clearly have been rummaging through sensitive files... and... stealing

personal property," the Broker explained, eyeing the snow globe that remained in Nate's hand.

As Nate slowly set the snow globe down on a nearby desk, Nick noticed one of the goons talking on an office phone.

"And when we show officers the security video, from select cameras of course, any claims you make about us will sound silly. Then you'll be put in jail, Mr. Myra, your companion here will be picked up by child protective services, and me and his friend over there will be able to enjoy the big Christmas present I promised him, along with an amazing view of the city. Isn't that right, Alex?" the Broker asked as he slightly turned his head but not his eyes.

"I'll be okay, Bug," Alex said, with a trembling voice that made his claim questionable. "Go with the police when they come. Just get out of here."

Nick tilted his head down toward Nate. "Bug?"

"It's just a nickname," Nate whispered, his eyes still fixed on the Broker. "Something my mom used to call me."

The Broker's gaze returned from a clock on the far wall. "You two have held us up long enough. Vince, Kyle, wait here with our unwelcome guests until the police arrive. You two, take the boy to the service elevator. Mr. Myra, 'Bug', happy holidays to you both."

As the menacing trio escorted Alex out of the office, the newly-arrived goons moved toward Nick and Nate with their own guns drawn, herding them toward a wall of lobby chairs.

"Let's not try anything stupid, you two," the bigger one advised. "We wouldn't want to have to tell the cops that you jumped us, and we were just defending ourselves, if you know what I mean."

CHAPTER 18:
WE'RE ON OUR WAY TO TOYLAND

Nate and his older associate had only been sitting for a few minutes when one of the Rching thugs started giving Nick a hard time. "I get why the kid's here, but how'd you get wrapped up in all this, old man? It's a little suspicious, don't you think, Kyle?" turning to his partner. "Who are you working for?"

"I serve the One who came at Christmas," Nick replied matter-of-factly.

The questioning captor moved even closer, hovering over the duo while brandishing his gun. "Trying to be funny? Notice I'm not laughing, grandpa."

As the goon tried to intimidate Nick, Nate carefully removed one of the supposedly-returned Christmas poppers from his jacket pocket. When the bully leaned in for another threatening remark, Nate made his move. As he twisted the cylinder's base, he thrust it up into the man's face. Just as the thug noticed the popper, it exploded in a puff of smoke and a huge cloud

of blue, white, and silver confetti. This took everyone by surprise... even Nick! But the very thing Nate hoped would happen happened: the surprised man stumbled backward into his partner, and both fell to the floor.

"Go, go, go!" yelled Nate wildly.

In a flash, the Christmas Eve companions raced through the door, down several hallways, following signs to the service elevator, swiping Guerrilla Gao's counterfeit card through every door.

"We might still be able to catch the men who took Alex," Nate suggested as they slid into the open elevator. "And... aren't you glad I kept a popper?" the young man asked, grinning.

"Let me think about that one" said Nick playfully. "But yes, hit the first floor button. If Alex is still nearby, they'll probably take him out through the loading dock."

As the old elevator lumbered downward, Nick and Nate looked at each other nervously. Given the elevator's speed, it may have been faster to escape down the back stairwell. Their fears were realized when the elevator doors opened at the exact same moment the two goons burst out of the stairwell door at the far end of a long corridor. A second later, the men spotted them.

"Quick. Press three!" Nick barked. The doors closed just before their pursuers arrived.

"They'll figure out we stopped on three, so we shouldn't stay in here. And we can't use the stairs," Nick explained as the doors reopened. "But when we came in, I saw a sign for a North Pole village on this level. Should be just out those doors. Let's hide in there until we can sneak down the toy store escalators and out the front doors."

Moments later, one of the Rching thugs, flashlight and gun in hand, cautiously crept through the North Pole village (the spot where shoppers could meet Santa and get a photo with him). As the still-out-of-breath goon searched for his escapees, he passed by the North Pole's central display, looking for any movement whatsoever, or anything out of the ordinary. What he surprisingly failed to notice among the costumed elf figures that surrounded Santa's chair was that one of them was Nate (wearing a borrowed elf hat), and even more conspicuous, that Nick (wearing another borrowed hat) was sitting perfectly still in the gilded chair at the center of it all. As the goon exited to an adjacent

room, Nick silently motioned to Nate, directing his attention to a large, spiral slide that apparently kids could ride down to the first floor after seeing  Santa Claus. Nate nodded his approval, and within seconds the two were sliding down, round and round, to the first floor. But the uneasy silence was broken as they attempted to sneak past the escalators toward the front doors.

"There they are! Stop or I'll shoot," yelled one of the goons as he bounded down the deactivated steps.

Thinking fast, Nate tipped over a tall barrel of colorful rubber balls. The Rching lackey couldn't stop himself before landing on the ball-covered floor, and winding up (again) on his back. Nate smiled as he and Nick burst through the front doors. But as they stumbled onto the sidewalk they were rudely met by a very bright light, and a blaring bullhorn. "This is the police! Get your hands in the air!"

CHAPTER 19:
SAY HELLO TO FRIENDS YOU KNOW, AND EVERYONE YOU MEET

s Nick and Nate, hands cuffed behind their backs, sat uncomfortably on the sidewalk next to the NYPD police cruiser, the Rching thug who moments earlier had been chasing them with a gun, was now chatting casually with one of the responding officers.

"Yes, we'd be happy to show you the video footage," the goon said calmly, casting a smug look toward the detained pair.

"Manny! I'm gonna head inside and take a look. You good here?" the taller cop said to his partner.

The second officer, who was standing just behind Nick and Nate, gave the duo a quick glance. "Yep. I think I can handle these two."

"A word of advice," the Rching guard commented as he and the officer backed  toward a door held open by his fellow goon, "Watch 'em like a hawk. Those two may look harmless, but they ain't."

As the men disappeared into the building, the companions sat quietly in the cold night air as some late and light Christmas Eve traffic motored by.

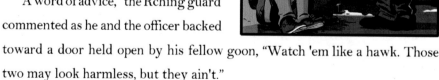

Nate squirmed uncomfortably, looking up at the cop (who was giving a brief response to police dispatch on his squawking radio).

"Those guys are the bad guys, not us," Nate growled. "They kidnapped my friend... and other kids!"

"Why don't you give me your name and address, or a phone number for a parent or guardian," the officer responded with a sincere smile, ignoring what must have sounded like wild claims.

"My parents are traveling and can't be reached," Nate said gruffly as his head dropped down. But within seconds, the boy's demeanor changed. "Look, this is my grandpa. He's been taking care of me. We saw these guys take my

friend Alex and so we followed them here. I'm afraid if we don't do something quickly, officer, I may never seem him again."

"Is that true, sir? Is that what happened?" the policeman asked shifting his focus to Nick.

"Well, you know what they say about the truth, Officer...?" Nick asked as he strained to see the name tag just below his badge.

"Quispe. Officer Quispe," the man responded.

"A pleasure to meet you, Officer Quispe. As I was saying, the truth..." Nick stopped mid-sentence as a look of confusion, then realization, washed over his face. "Quispe? If I'm not mistaken, that's a Quechua name. Is your family from northern or southern Peru?"

"Yeah, Quechua," answered the surprised cop. "My grandparents are from northern Peru."

"Quispe," Nick repeated as he looked up and off. "And three generations in New York City. Why I am surprised," he added with a huge grin and a booming chuckle.

"I'm not sure I understand what you're getting at, Mister..." the policemen stated as he looked down at Nick's wallet and driver's license. "Mr. Myra".

"This may be hard to believe, but what I'm getting at, Officer Quispe, is related to your great-grandmother, or maybe a great aunt," Nick replied excitedly. "Does this phrase mean anything to you? 'When Nick knocks...'?"

Minutes later Nick and Nate, freed from their restraints, were walking briskly around the backside of the Randolph Building.

"But why isn't he coming with us? We need help," Nate argued as he repeatedly looked back.

"He was reluctant enough to simply release us, let alone come with us. But he'll buy us some time when those Rching fellows return. For now, we've got to get back inside that building," Nick answered as he craned his neck, looking up the side of the iconic structure. As the two rounded the corner to the loading docks, the man in red retrieved the counterfeit access card from a secret pocket in his jacket.

"But weren't they taking Alex someplace else?" Nate asked. "You think he's still in the building?"

"Not in the building," responded Nick. "On top of it."

CHAPTER 20:
NOT A CREATURE WAS STIRRING, NOT EVEN A MOUSE?

don't know what they're doing up there," confessed Nick as the persistent pair crept up through a rooftop access stairwell tucked in the back corner of the thirty-eighth floor. "But I'm sure that's where they are. Remember? The Broker said something about promising Alex a big Christmas present and an amazing view of the city. And there is literally a giant Christmas present on top of this building."

When they arrived at the access door, Nick carefully leaned his head out, praying no one was standing nearby. He didn't need to lean far before catching sight of Alex and the Broker on the opposite side of the roof, just behind and under the massive, wrapped gift box sitting at the far end of the toy store's neon sign. Thankfully, the Broker was facing away from everyone else, and the two goons who had accompanied him and the boy were nowhere to be found. So as he and Nate crept out onto the roof (with noise from the city below masking the sound of their steps), Nick began waving his hands in the air, hoping to get

Alex's attention. But instead of seeing Nick and then sneaking away, Alex first noticed his friend. And without thinking, he excitedly blurted out, "Bug!". It was enough to get the Broker's attention, who lunged for a pistol sitting nearby and grabbed Alex from behind.

"Stop right there," shouted the Broker, as he moved the gun back and forth between his captive and the problematic pair. "It seems, Mr. Myra, that you two have foolishly reinserted yourself into the equation."

"If your equation involves hurting children, I'll do everything I can to rewrite the equation," Nick replied confidently.

The Broker, squinting behind his small, round spectacles, quickly looked back and up, then around at the rest of the roof. "Here's what's going to happen, Mr. Myra. You'll keep your distance, and my young friend and I will be headed out that door behind you. I wouldn't want to have to hurt the boy. But I will if I must. And if I must, then you'll force me to take your companion instead," the Broker said as he buried the pistol in Alex's side. "One way or another, I will meet my quota."

In response, Nick, his eyes fixed on the Broker, stepped even more in front of Nate, widening his stance. But Nate was looking past the bad guy to, of all things, a rat sitting on the far ledge. As the Broker began to move to his left, clockwise along the back of the huge sign and toward the access door, Nick and Nate began moving to their left, around the back edge of the roof. When Nate realized they were trading places, an idea came to him. Out of his coat pocket he slipped the one Christmas cookie he had taken from the

Lepps earlier that evening. As they slowly moved along the roof's edge, and with the cookie hidden in his hand, Nate (partially hidden behind Nick) began chipping off small pieces with his thumb onto the ledge. When the pairs had finally swapped spots, Nate whispered to his new friend.

"Get him talking before they leave," Nate advised, in a way that confirmed he had a plan. Nick nodded, ever so slightly.

"Sooner or later it will happen," shouted Nick, just before the Broker turned toward the door.

"And what exactly will happen, Mr. Myra," the Broker asked smugly.

"Men like you will answer for your crimes."

"Men like me?" the Broker replied. "You mean businessmen? That's all this is, sir. Business. That's all life is. Business. And you either profit or you pay. I choose profit. And what's profitable for me now is to take my leave of you. So unless you want someone to get hurt, please don't try to follow us."

Before the man could turn away, Nate spoke up. "I'll miss you, Alex. All of us will... including Mr. Beady Eyes. Remember him? When you need him, just reach out to him."

Alex, who was closer to the edge of the roof, had to think for a moment about his friend's strange farewell. But it made sense when he glanced over and noticed the rat on the ledge to his left (the rat who had followed Nate's trail of crumbs around to where it started). Within seconds, the Broker (who didn't know what to make of Nate's goodbye) was caught off guard as Alex courageously grabbed the rat and thrust it into his captor's face. Apparently convinced he needed both his hands to remove the rat (who was now clinging to his glasses), the man released Alex, dropped the gun, and stumbled backwards, scraping frantically at his face... as he fell over the edge of the roof.

CHAPTER 21:
FORTH THEY
WENT TOGETHER

hough Nick and Nate had just seen the Broker fall backwards over the edge of the Randolph Building's roof, they quickly found themselves dealing with a very relieved, but still trembling Alex. As the boy's tears mixed with laughter, the Christmas Eve comrades reassured him that he was now safe. But what about the Broker? By the time Nick was able to inspect the edge over which the scoundrel fell, it had been almost a minute. When he finally did, he was shocked to discover that a smaller, narrow roof ran along the backside of the building, at least two floors below the main roof.

But the Broker was nowhere to be seen. Instead, an access hatch (about ten feet or so from where the Broker must have landed) was open, with the top of a metal ladder visible from Nick's vantage point.

Minutes later, at the exact opposite end of the building, Detective Jason Alonso arrived to find Officer Quispe standing out front, waiting for his partner. Officer Quispe had been rehearsing what he might say in order to explain the apparent escape of his two suspects.

"So you were responding to a call that involved a boy and an older gentleman with a bushy white beard breaking into an office?" the detective asked.

"Yes sir," responded Quispe, his head and eyes lowered as he fumbled through his notepad. "The Rching Security office."

"And you ended up just letting them go because, in your words, 'something didn't add up'?"

"Yes sir," Quispe replied. "You see, when we first saw them, they came bursting through those doors..."

At that very moment, as if scripted, Nick, Nate, and Alex excitedly rushed through the very same doors.

"Actually... it happened just like that," remarked the stunned police officer.

When Nick caught sight of Detective Alonso standing next to the squad car, he shot a waving hand into the air, as his eyes and smile widened (like someone motioning to an old friend across a crowded room).

"Detective Alonso! Am I glad to see you," Nick shouted. "This is the boy we told you about; the one who had been abducted. But the man who just held him at gunpoint, the man behind all of this, has escaped. Officer Quispe, did you see a slender man in a suit, with dark, slicked-back hair, come out of the building?"

"Actually, I did. Just a couple minutes before you arrived, Detective," Quispe replied. "He looked injured. But before I could say anything, he stumbled south on Payne, talking on his cell phone."

"Officer, get a statement from this young man," directed Alonso, with a hand on Alex's shoulder. He then turned to Nick and Nate. "You two, hop in my car. Let's see if we can track this guy down. If injured, he couldn't have gotten far."

Moments later, Nate and the two men were carefully exploring the adjacent streets. As each of them peered intently through the car windows, hoping to spot the escaping villain, Nick broke the silence.

"I'm curious about how you ended up at the Randolph Building, Detective."

"It was because of that van, Mr. Myra; the one you encountered earlier. When I interviewed the actual owner of the vehicle, he had video footage that showed one of the thieves wearing a Rching security jacket. I recognized it because I investigated the company a couple years back. Even though the investigation hit a dead end, it continued to bother me. So you believe these guys are behind the abductions?"

"I know they are," Nick replied, as he continued to scan the street to his right. "But apart from Alex, we couldn't find any trace of the kids. The man we're looking for, this 'Broker', he knows where they are. We have to find him."

"Like I said, he couldn't have gotten far," Alonso emphasized. "Most of these buildings and businesses are closed up because of the holiday. If he got off the street, I'm not sure where..."

"A church," Nate blurted out. "Some churches are always open, especially on Christmas Eve, right?"

Detective Alonso looked at Nate. His expression was dismissive at first. But as his face changed, his foot slammed down on the gas pedal.

"There's a church two blocks over with a midnight service," Alonso explained. "I did after-hours security there a few times when I was a beat cop. It's big, old, dark, and currently open. In short, a good place to hide out on Christmas Eve."

CHAPTER 22:
THEN ENTERED IN THOSE WISE MEN THREE

s the detective's car pulled up in front of the old church, a small group of people were visiting on the sidewalk out front. The midnight service would be starting in about thirty minutes, and some in the group seemed to be waiting for family or friends to arrive. As Jason Alonso scanned up and down the sidewalk, he noticed someone in the shadows, just behind the bundled-up service goers.

"That may be our man," the detective said calmly.

"Where?" asked Nick.

"Right behind that group, against the wall. But I think he just noticed my car."

Sure enough, the Broker limped out of the shadows with his head down, and ducked through the church's front door.

"That was him alright," Nick said confidently. "Should we wait for backup?"

"If by 'we' you mean you and the boy, then yes. Please wait here, Mr. Myra. I'll call it in. But I need to make sure he doesn't go out another way."

"Again, call me 'Nick'. Are you sure about going in?" Nick asked as he then looked around. "He could have his own backup coming to this very location."

"Nick, I realized tonight that I've been sitting things out for far too long. I can't explain it, but somehow all of this is connected. Me. You. That van. Rching. The kids. This church. Someone tonight reminded me about the importance of hope. Well, I have to believe things can get better, and that I can still make a difference in seeing that they do. So I *hope* you'll wait here," Alonso added with a smirk. "And I *hope* you'll lock the doors."

With that the detective stepped out of the car, radio in hand. Nick and Nate watched as he steered away from the crowd while communicating with his dispatcher. After looking up and down the street, he casually entered the church.

"So we're really just gonna sit here," Nate asked, not hiding his frustration.

Instead of responding, Nick simply looked down at his watch. He was clearly thinking.

"Fine. Can you at least open this back door? I need to use the bathroom. There's a porta-potty right across the street at that work site."

"Alright. Just be quick about it," answered Nick, looking again at his watch before he got out and opened the rear door of the unmarked police cruiser. As he did, Nate stepped out onto the sidewalk and went around the back of the car, looking as if he were about to cross the street. But instead, he simply strolled around the driver's side of the vehicle (while Nick followed him with his eyes). As he came around the front of the car he glanced over at Nick, then ran straight into the church.

Once inside the narthex, Nate could see a choir through the main sanctuary doors. He could also hear them as they practiced a Christmas carol.

"Away in a manger, no crib for a bed."

Nate slipped in along the back wall to listen, forgetting for a moment why he was there. It was his mom's favorite Christmas song. She sang it every year in the weeks leading up to Christmas, especially the Christmas before she died. His heart began to hurt. He wished she was here. He wished he could have made her better. He wished they didn't have to leave Nate's dad. He wished he wasn't alone. It was that final thought that brought him back around. He wasn't alone. He had friends, and his friends were still in trouble. Maybe, just maybe, they were here, hidden some- where in the building.

Maybe that's why the Broker came to this church. He had to be sure. As he crept out of the sanctuary through a side door, he found himself in a hallway that ran alongside the main building. Within seconds, he noticed that a door at the far end of the hallway was open just slightly. As Nate slowly moved through the cracked door, he discovered a dimly lit stairwell. Suddenly he heard the door close behind him, felt a hand on his shoulder, and flinched as what he assumed was a gun was pressed into his back.

"Well, well. If it isn't that pesky 'Bug'. It looks like I'll be meeting my quota after all."

CHAPTER 23:
SIRE, THE NIGHT
IS DARKER NOW

ot wanting to alarm those in attendance, Jason Alonso put on a halfway decent smile and moved as casually as he could from one part of the church building to another. Knowing Nick was watching the front, the detective found that every other exit door he could locate was locked or was equipped with a fire alarm. If the man had left the building, he would have known about it. Only one other area remained unchecked: the bell tower. He had been up there once before, many Christmases ago while doing after-hours security work. So he made his way to a musty storage closet and to an old, metal ladder tucked in its corner. He carefully lifted the dusty half-door in the closet's ceiling and began to climb. As he moved past a series of openings that vented the church's attic, he was surprised to hear the practicing choir even more clearly than in other parts of the building.

"What child is this who, laid to rest, on Mary's lap is sleeping?"

When Detective Alonso reached the trap door at the top of the ladder, he listened for any sounds of activity. Hearing nothing, he lifted the door just enough to scan the old, wooden floor. Seeing nothing, Alonso again lifted the door and climbed up just enough to gently set it down, fully open. The tall tower that once held bells was now filled with speakers (to simulate chiming bells) and with cell phone transmitters. As Alonso climbed into the space, he slowly drew his sidearm, and at the same time, slowly drew in a deep breath of the cold night air. Just as he exhaled, the detective heard a muffled cry behind him. Spinning around, he saw the Broker step out from

behind an array of transmitters. Nate was positioned in front of him, a gun in his back and the scoundrel's hand over his mouth.

"I remember you," said the Broker smugly. "Your the detective who gave us trouble a couple years back. And now, here you are again, failing just as badly." Though mixed with noise from the encircling city, the sound of the choir once again could be heard through the open trap door.

"What child is this..."

"Backup is on the way. Let the boy go. He has nothing to do with this," Alonso ordered calmly, as he, weapon raised, began to move to his right, away from the trap door.

"Oh he has everything to do with this. He's why we're here. Isn't that right, Bug?"

Alonso flinched. "Why did he call you that?" asked the shaken detective, looking intently at Nate.

The curious Broker moved his hand from Nate's mouth and placed it on his shoulder.

"Um," stammered Nate, "because... it's what my mom used to call me."

"And... what's your mom's name?" Alonso asked gruffly. "Isn't your last name 'Washington'?"

"What child is this..."

"Keep your distance, Detective," the Broker warned as Alonso continued moving around the tower.

"Kid, what's your mom's name," Alonso asked again. "And... how old are you?"

"Her name was... Aubrey," Nate answered, clearly confused about the 'why' behind these questions.

Alonso looked stunned. Not only by what Nate was telling him, but also by the sight of Nick's head slowly rising up through the trap  door opening. Thankfully, the Broker was too intrigued by the detective's questions and lack of composure to notice Nick.

"I'd love to know where this line of questioning is leading," the Broker interjected, "but Bug and I have two helicopter seats with our names on them. It should be here any minute. Yes, it will be risky climbing aboard from the roof of this tower, but I know you wouldn't do anything to make it even riskier for the boy. Isn't that right, Detective?"

By this time, Nick had somehow stealthily made his way behind the Broker. After a quick scan, he used three fingers to rapidly jab the man's lower back, just next to his spine. In an instant, the villain's right side seemed to go limp, and he began to crumple to the floor. At the same moment, Nick grabbed Nate with his left arm and pushed him backward, out of the way. But as the Broker fell, he began to spin to his right. As he did, somehow, before he hit the floor, he managed to get one shot off. In an instant, Alonso and Nate watched helplessly as Nick also crumpled to the floor, clutching his stomach.

CHAPTER 24:
SOON IT WILL BE CHRISTMAS DAY

s the sound of police sirens began to converge on the old church, Detective Jason Alonso (after disarming and handcuffing the Broker) rushed to the corner of the tower where a distraught Nate was kneeling over a groaning Nick, still clutching his stomach.

"We have to stop the bleeding," Nate said frantically, as he removed the knit beanie from his head.

"Well... I don't see any blood. Do you?" the detective asked as he looked Nick over.

The tower interior was dark, so Nate had to look very carefully. "Actually, no. But how? We saw you get shot."

Nick, who had his eyes closed and was laying flat on his back, suddenly opened them and began to feel his stomach. He then began to pat his coat. His eyes widened, and he slowly reached in and removed his silver pocket watch... which now had a bullet lodged directly in its center. Nate and Alonso gasped at the same time.

"You're one lucky guy, Mr. Myra," the detective concluded.

"I don't believe in luck, Detective Alonso," Nick retorted, still looking at the silver watch.

"Okay, but I know that left a bruise," Alonso commented. "That's probably what you're feeling. By the way, how in the world did you get the jump on that guy?"

"Ah. I used a couple techniques I picked up in feudal Japan," Nick explained, as he carefully tried to position himself against the side wall. "The 'quiet grasshopper' walk and the 'hidden hornet' jab. It causes partial paralysis for a few seconds. A hard move to perfect. I'm glad it finally worked." He looked back to Nate and added a wink. Nate, once again, rolled his eyes and shook his head.

"But seeing as I've literally lost time, I'm guessing I only have a few more minutes," Nick added.

"Whaddya mean, 'a few more minutes'?" Nate asked. "You're gonna be okay, right?"

"Yes, I will be okay, Nate," Nick responded reassuringly. "But remember what I told you. My time here is almost over. Soon, I will wake up somewhere else, in order to help someone else."

Nate certainly remembered what Nick had told him in the Rching office about his divine mission in the past, but he hadn't stopped to consider what it meant for the present. For *his* present. As everything became clear and real, he was suddenly overcome with emotion.

"No. Please don't leave," Nate pleaded. "I just met you. I just... I... I need someone... I..."

Nick, tears in eyes, pulled the boy close. "It will be okay, child. You will see me again. And... you won't be alone. Don't you understand? I was over-

joyed to help Alex, and I know you'll find the others. But you were the mission, Nate. I came here for you... and for the Detective.

Please, tell him, Jason," Nick requested as he shifted his gaze to the detective, who was kneeling down next to him.

"Well," Alonso explained, attempting to sort his emotions, "I... I think you're my son, Nate."

Nate's face went from shocked to sad to thrilled to angry in an instant. "No, we had to leave my dad. He wasn't a good person. He didn't care about my mom. He wanted to send her away."

"No, I wanted her to get help, Nathan," Alonso replied, tears welling up in his eyes. "You must have known she was sick. Her mind. The drugs. She needed help. But she wouldn't admit it. She was scared. And then... she ran. And she took you with her. You were so little. Her little 'Bug'. But I couldn't find you. Believe me, I tried, for a long time. "

"No... If... You should have kept looking," Nate responded. "I didn't know what to do."

"I'm so sorry, Nathan. I thought you died in a fire, son. But you're right. I shouldn't have given up."

"And you won't," Nick interjected. "I know you won't. Not ever again. You were right, Detective. All of this is connected. You were right to hope. 'Do not fear, only believe.'"

After so many centuries, Nick knew the 'midnight feeling' as it approached. His eyes would grow heavy, but his body felt light. With one last glance he smiled at the father and son he'd help reunite, and whispered a prayer of gratitude. As the speakers sounded the simulated bells, tolling that Christmas had arrived, the man in red simply faded away. Only the silver pocket watch remained.

CHAPTER 25:
SO THIS IS CHRISTMAS

e wrote me a note," Alonso explained to Nate. "It must have been when he—when you—were sitting out in front of the church. I think think he realized he was running out of time."

"I don't understand," admitted Nate. "What did he say?"

"He said he figured it out. The Gift Exchange. The invoices for medical supplies that he had found. It was why the Broker had Alex on the roof last night. The abducted kids, your friends, were inside that giant present. It was outfitted with bunks and restraints and equipment to keep the kids sedated."

"But why? What were they going to do with them?"

"Well, a couple of the guys we arrested told us that when the helicopter comes later this week to remove the giant gift box, they were going to fly the kids out to a boat waiting in international waters. Law enforcement has made trafficking a lot harder through the ports and roadways, so this was their elaborate attempt to avoid those measures. Pretty crazy."

"And we were right there on the roof, and didn't even know it," Nate sighed.

The newly reunited father and son both looked up toward the top of the Randolph Building. The first light of morning (Christmas morning to be exact) was beginning to cover the city, and law enforcement and emergency vehicles covered the surrounding streets. Nate, a cup of hot chocolate in his hands, sat in the back of a police cruiser, while the detective knelt down next to the open door.

"They're bringing the kids down as we speak. Sounds like all of them are going to be okay," Alonso explained while still looking up. "They do need to take them to the hospital, just to make sure. Maybe we can go over and see them later. How does that sound?"

"It sounds like a good idea," answered Nate, also still looking up. "I'm glad they're okay."

"I was going to mention something about counseling services being available for them (for all of you), but I think *I* may need to talk with someone even sooner," confessed the detective. "It messes with your head when you see a guy just fade away in front of you."

"Yep. Weird. Super weird," added Nate.

"But if what you told me is true about who he is, then I guess it makes sense. It changes things though, right?"

"Yeah. But in a good way," said Nate. "Life feels bigger. More... meaningful? Is that the right word? Makes me want to understand it better."

"You're a sharp kid, Nathan. By the way, in case you didn't know, your full name is Nathan Christopher Alonso. Christopher was my dad's dad." Nate simply nodded in acknowledgment, trying to take it all in. "You know, that raises the question: where did the name 'Washington' come from?"

"For a while, I guess when we first left, Mom and I lived in and around Washington Square Park. That must have been when she changed it. I knew it wasn't really our name, since she would also refer to herself as Aubrey Harper."

"That was her maiden name," Alonso explained. "But I could never locate her with either 'Alonso' or 'Harper'. She worked hard not to be found. Can... can I ask you how she died?"

"It was a few years ago. I was younger, but I think it was an overdose."

"I can't imagine how hard that must have been. I wish I could have been there for you."

"I know. I think I'm beginning to understand that," said Nate.

"But please know I will be there for you now, Nate. And that won't change, just like Nick said."

"I wonder," Nate remarked, turning his head toward the rising sun, "I wonder where he's going to wake up this time."

"I don't know," answered Nate's dad, "but wherever it is, I know it's exactly where he's supposed to be."

"I think I'm beginning to understand that as well," said Nate, warmed on that cold Christmas morning by the fresh memory of an unexpected friendship.

EPILOGUE:

As Nate attempted to fall asleep on the creaky, pull-out sofa bed in the front room of his dad's apartment, his exhausted body simply tossed and turned. Christmas Day had almost run its course, but his thoughts were still racing at full speed. Specifically, he was playing back in his head, over and over again, the events of the previous evening. "All of it actually happened, right?" he asked himself. "Or was it just a dream?" The fact he was currently laying in an NYPD detective's apartment helped reassure him of the answer he already and ultimately knew to be true. As he turned to look again at the clock, another item came to mind in terms of reassurance. He reached across to the chair on which his jacket was hung and dug out of the left pocket the silver watch that had remained, even when Nick had disappeared; the silver pocket watch that had saved Nick's life. The first thing he noticed when he held the watch up to the light (from a nearby window) was the bullet hole just above six o'clock. He remembered that when Nick faded away, the watch fell to the ground, knocking the embedded bullet loose. But the second thing he noticed was something he hadn't noticed before. Through the hole, amongst the watch's gears and springs, Nate observed what looked like the end of a small, old-fashioned key. Though he didn't want to damage the watch any more, he decided to see if he could remove the back of the watch. He tried very carefully until, finally, the intricate inner workings of the watch were revealed. Sure enough, placed in the middle of its many mechanisms was a small silver key. He hesitated to pull it loose. Turning on a nearby lamp instead, he examined the watch in the light and quickly noticed very small symbols etched into the head of the key. As he looked from the watch to the city beyond the window, Nate was dealing with new questions: "What might these symbols mean? Did Nick know about this key?" Above all, "What did this key open?" He didn't know how he would answer these questions, but he was determined to find a way.